christmas cocktails

christmas cocktails

50 RECIPES FOR HOLIDAY CELEBRATIONS AND MAKING SPIRITS BRIGHT

camille wilson

photography by neetu laddha

TEN SPEED PRESS
California | New York

contents

INTRODUCTION 9

SANTA'S WORKSHOP 13

TOOLS 15

GLASSWARE 16

HOMEMADE HOLIDAY SYRUPS 20

COCKTAIL RIMS 31

FESTIVE HOLIDAY GARNISHES 34

SCALING UP YOUR COCKTAILS 37

HOLIDAY CLASSICS 41

CHRISTMAS IN THE TROPICS 61

WARM UP THIS WINTER 85

PARTY PERFECT PUNCHES 105

NAUGHTY AND NICE 125

INDEX 139

introduction

Christmas has always been a special holiday for me. Growing up as part of a large family meant it was a holiday full of magic, due in large part to the traditions my parents created. One of those traditions was Christmas dinner. Christmas dinner at my parents' home was and still is one of my favorite traditions. It's a day full of love, laughter, delicious food, and a house packed wall-to-wall with cousins, aunts, uncles, friends, and other loved ones. It is chaotic in the best way and, most importantly, so memorable.

Christmas dinner is like the Super Bowl for my parents. They start prepping days in advance—seasoning, stirring, marinating. Then, the morning of, the house is filled with aromas of curries and spices and reggae holiday classics blasting through the living room speakers. Guests travel from near and far. And when they arrive, the house echoes with laughter, jokes, and unbelievable stories about their childhoods in the islands. At the end of the night, people leave into the cold with full bellies, warm hearts, and to-go plates. So when I started writing this book, I knew I wanted the recipes to evoke that same love and warmth I get to experience year after year at Mommy and Daddy's Christmas dinner.

The pages of this book are full of cocktail recipes that will get you in the holiday spirit. Think cozy classics with a twist and flavors like cinnamon, vanilla, nutmeg, and cranberry, to name a few. But it's also more than just a recipe book. It's a love letter to my favorite holiday. It's a tribute to the traditions I grew up with—sipping sorrel, slicing black cake, secret Santa—and the ones I'm still creating.

Looking back, I realize that my parents' Christmas dinner taught me a lot of lessons about the art of gathering and what it means to create a warm, welcoming home and lasting impressions. Through them, I got to witness genuine hospitality and authentic connection. So in addition to the cocktail recipes, you'll also find some of my best tips and tricks for creating memorable experiences for your guests. Paired with the cocktails in this book, my holiday hosting hacks will inspire you to see hosting with fresh eyes and make you excited to shake and stir up Christmas magic your guests will never forget.

My hope for you is that you'll find recipes you will want to make for yourselves and your loved ones over and over again. And that you'll revisit these pages every holiday season to find joy and inspiration. Who knows? It may even spark ideas for your next holiday tradition.

But no matter what your holiday traditions are, I hope you'll join me on this journey of creating Christmas magic through cocktails. So here's to clinking glasses in good company during Christmastime and beyond!

the gift of cocktails

When attending a holiday party, bringing a gift for the host is a thoughtful way to show your appreciation. A bottle of wine or bubbly is always a safe bet. But if you want to go the extra mile and do something even more thoughtful and creative, the DIY Cocktail Kit is a clever and memorable way to say thank you.

First, select the cocktail you'd like to gift—it could be a favorite cocktail of theirs or an original cocktail recipe you've developed on your own (mimosas work really well for this). Next, identify and portion out the cocktail ingredients. For an elevated presentation, use stylish, gift-worthy containers like mason jars or swing-top bottles. Then, add the ingredients to a gift bag or box. Finally, add a printed or handwritten recipe card to seal the deal.

Cole

santa's workshop

welcome cocktails

Offering your guests a welcome cocktail when they arrive to your gathering is a great way to set the tone for your party. It also gives people a sneak peek of what's to come. If you have a theme, this is the perfect place to introduce it. After navigating planes, trains, and rideshares to get to your party, guests will appreciate a thoughtful libation the moment they walk in. I like to serve mine in mini glasses and place them on a tray so guests can grab them upon arrival.

For me, there's no greater gift than having people re-create my cocktail recipes at home. But I recognize that readers may be at different levels in their home bartender journeys. So, in order to set you up for success, I'm laying out some mixology fundamentals in this chapter, as well as syrup recipes, fun garnish ideas, and more.

TOOLS

To masterfully create the seasonal cocktails in this book, having the proper tools is key. Below you'll find a comprehensive list of the tools needed to mix and shake every recipe. You'll also find a few alternatives if you don't have the tools listed on hand.

BAR SPOON A bar spoon comes in handy for cocktails whose ingredients are stirred. A kitchen spoon or butter knife are great alternatives.

CITRUS PRESS Many recipes call for fresh lemon or lime juice; a citrus press will make juicing lemons and limes fast and easy.

COCKTAIL SHAKER A tool used to combine liquid ingredients. When used with ice, the cocktail shaker also helps chill your cocktail to its optimal temperature. There are several different types of cocktail shakers on the market. I recommend using a cobbler shaker, also known as a three-piece cocktail shaker, which has a strainer built in. The strainer will come in handy for drinks that are served without ice in a coupe or martini glass.

JIGGER An essential bar tool used to measure liquid ingredients. This tool will assist you in keeping your drinks balanced and consistent. You can also use measuring spoons or measuring cups to ensure precise measurements in lieu of a jigger.

MESH STRAINER A tool that separates solids from liquids in the cocktail-making process. A number of the cocktails in this book are served up, meaning that they are shaken with ice and then served without ice. A mesh strainer will assist you in keeping the ice out of the glass. It's especially helpful for cocktails with herbs or fruit, allowing you to strain out any solid bits to enjoy a perfectly smooth sip. For recipes that call for a double strain, you can use your mesh strainer along with the strainer built into your cocktail shaker or a Hawthorne Strainer to achieve this.

MIXING GLASS A mixing glass is a vessel used to combine liquid ingredients—usually with ice—before straining into a glass and serving. When used in conjunction with a bar spoon, it allows for smooth, controlled stirring that chills and dilutes the drink. You can use the tin or base of your cocktail shaker as an alternative.

MUDDLER A muddler is used to macerate ingredients like fresh fruits and herbs. Its blunt edge helps to smash solid ingredients. A mortar and pestle set serve as a great alternative if you don't have a muddler at home.

GLASSWARE

The cocktails in this book will delight you whether you sip them out of the proper glassware or not. For me, serving drinks in gorgeous vessels is part of the experience and can really elevate your happy-hour-at-home experience. Here are a few suggestions of glassware to have on hand to get the most out of the recipes in this book.

CHAMPAGNE FLUTE A tall glass on a long stem that's used to hold sparkling wine cocktails without ice. They typically hold 6 to 10 ounces of liquid and are perfect for drinks like mimosas and French 75s.

COPPER MUG A wide, round metal vessel with a handle that's used to hold cocktails served with ice. They typically hold around 12 to 20 ounces of liquid. Mules, which are cocktails topped with ginger beer, are typically served in a copper mug.

festive glassware

Adding a little pizzazz to your glassware is an easy way to level up your next gathering. A few simple touches can really elevate any soiree.

RIBBONS Tie a ribbon to your stemware to dress them up. You can use a variety of colors or textures of ribbon depending on the look you're hoping to achieve. Plus they double as handy drink markers so guests know which one is their glass!

GOLD FLAKES Adorn the rim of your glass with edible gold flakes for a festive pop. (See page 31 for more detailed instructions.)

DRIED EDIBLE FLOWERS Dried edible flowers (like rose petals, hibiscus leaves, lavender, etc.) can add a pop of color and a lovely aroma to the rim of your cocktail glass. As with gold flakes, brush a bit of honey on the rim of your glass so the flowers have something to adhere to.

COUPE GLASS A bowl-shaped glass on a long stem that's used to hold cocktails or spirits without ice. They typically hold around 4 to 8 ounces of liquid. Cocktails like daiquiris, martinis, and sidecars are typically served in coupe glasses.

HEAT-RESISTANT GLASS A vessel with a handle that can be used to serve hot beverages. In this book there are a number of warm beverages, so a drinking vessel with a handle will help you hold your warm beverage without fear of being burned.

HIGHBALL GLASS A tall, slim glass that holds about 8 to 12 ounces of liquid. It's sometimes used in place of a Collins glass. Cocktails like highballs, Dark 'n' Stormys, and Long Island iced teas are typically served in highball glasses.

LOWBALL GLASS A short, wide tumbler used to hold cocktails or spirits with ice; also known as a rocks glass or Old-Fashioned glass. They typically hold around 2 to 10 ounces of liquid and are used for cocktails like Negronis, margaritas, and Old-Fashioneds.

MARTINI GLASS A triangle-shaped glass on a long stem that's used to hold cocktails served without ice. Ideal for drinks like martinis and cosmos, martini glasses typically hold 6 to 10 ounces of liquid.

PITCHER A large vessel used to serve batched drinks like punches and sangrias.

RED WINE GLASS A large bowl-shaped glass on a long stem that's used to hold wine or cocktails served with ice. Wine glasses hold 12 to 16 ounces of liquid and are great for serving punch or sangrias.

HOMEMADE HOLIDAY SYRUPS

For swirling into many of the drinks you'll find in this book—syrups add a boost of flavor without a lot of effort.

simple syrup

MAKES 1½ CUPS

1 cup granulated sugar

In a small saucepan over medium heat, combine the sugar and 1 cup water. Stir until the sugar is dissolved. Remove from the heat and let cool. Transfer to a resealable container. Store in the refrigerator for up to 4 weeks.

spiced syrup

MAKES 1½ CUPS

- 1 cup packed brown sugar
- ½ cup peeled and chopped fresh ginger
- 2 cloves
- 3 cinnamon sticks

In a small saucepan over medium heat, combine the brown sugar and 1 cup water. Stir until the sugar is dissolved. Add the ginger, cloves, and cinnamon sticks. Stir to combine. Cover and bring to a light boil. Turn the heat to low and simmer for 15 minutes. Remove from the heat and let cool. Strain into a resealable container, discarding the solids. Store in the refrigerator for up to 2 weeks.

spiced cranberry syrup

MAKES 1½ CUPS

1 cup granulated sugar
1 cup cranberries
1 tablespoon allspice
2 cinnamon sticks
Peel from 1 orange

In a small saucepan over medium heat, combine the sugar and 1 cup water. Stir until the sugar is dissolved. Add the cranberries, allspice, cinnamon sticks, and orange peel. Cover and bring to a light boil. Turn the heat to low and simmer for 10 minutes. Remove from the heat and let cool. Strain into a resealable container and use a spoon to squeeze out any remaining juice from the cranberries, then discard the solids. Store in the refrigerator for up to 2 weeks.

pistachio syrup

MAKES 1½ CUPS

1 cup granulated sugar
1 cup shelled and chopped pistachios

In a small saucepan over medium heat, combine the sugar and 1 cup water. Stir until the sugar is dissolved. Add the pistachios. Cover and bring to a light boil. Turn the heat to low and simmer for 10 minutes. Remove from the heat and let cool. Strain into a resealable container, discarding the solids. Store in the refrigerator for up to 2 weeks.

hibiscus honey syrup

MAKES 1½ CUPS

1 cup dried hibiscus leaves
¾ cup honey

In a small saucepan over medium heat, combine the dried hibiscus leaves, honey, and 1 cup water. Stir to combine. Cover and bring to a light boil. Turn the heat to low and simmer for 10 minutes. Remove from the heat and let cool. Strain into a resealable container, discarding the solids. Store in the refrigerator for up to 2 weeks.

toasted marshmallow syrup

MAKES 1½ CUPS

7 to 8 large marshmallows
1 cup granulated sugar

Toast the marshmallows on the stovetop or with a kitchen torch and set aside. In a small saucepan over medium heat, combine the sugar and 1 cup water. Stir until the sugar is dissolved, then add the toasted marshmallows. Stir until the marshmallows are dissolved. Remove from the heat and let cool. Strain into a resealable container, discarding any solids. Store in the refrigerator for up to 2 weeks.

basil syrup

MAKES 1½ CUPS

1 cup granulated sugar
1 cup basil leaves

In a small saucepan over medium heat, combine the sugar, basil, and 1 cup water and bring to a light boil. Lower the heat and simmer for 1 minute. Remove from the heat and let steep, covered, for 30 minutes. Strain into a resealable container, discarding the solids. Store in the refrigerator for up to 2 weeks.

cinnamon syrup

MAKES 1½ CUPS

1 cup granulated sugar
3 cinnamon sticks

In a small saucepan over medium heat, combine the sugar, cinnamon sticks, and 1 cup water and bring to a boil. Once boiling, lower the heat and simmer for 5 minutes. Remove from the heat and let steep, covered, for 30 minutes. Strain into a resealable container, discarding the solids. Store in the refrigerator for up to 2 weeks.

ginger syrup

MAKES 1½ CUPS

1 cup granulated sugar
1 cup peeled and chopped fresh ginger

In a small saucepan over medium heat, combine the sugar and 1 cup water. Stir until the sugar is dissolved, then add the ginger. Bring the mixture to a low boil. Remove from the heat and let steep for 1 hour. Strain into a resealable container, discarding the solids. Store in the refrigerator for up to 2 weeks.

blackberry syrup

MAKES 1½ CUPS

1 cup granulated sugar
1 cup whole blackberries

In a small saucepan over medium heat, combine the sugar and 1 cup water. Stir until the sugar is dissolved. Add the blackberries. Cover and bring to a low boil. Turn the heat to low and simmer for 10 minutes. Remove from the heat and let cool. Strain into a resealable container, using a spoon to squeeze out any remaining juice from the blackberries, then discard the solids. Store in the refrigerator for up to 2 weeks.

orange ginger syrup

MAKES 1½ CUPS

1 cup granulated sugar
1 cup orange juice
½ cup peeled and chopped fresh ginger

In a small saucepan over medium heat, combine the sugar and orange juice. Stir until the sugar is dissolved. Add the ginger. Cover and bring to a light boil. Turn the heat to low and simmer for 15 minutes. Remove from the heat and let cool. Strain into a resealable container, discarding any solids. Store in the refrigerator for up to 2 weeks.

spiced apple syrup

MAKES 1½ CUPS

1 cup packed brown sugar
1 cup chopped apples
¼ teaspoon ground nutmeg
2 cinnamon sticks

In a small saucepan over medium heat, combine the brown sugar and 1 cup water. Stir until the sugar is dissolved. Add the apples, nutmeg, and cinnamon sticks. Cover and bring to a light boil. Turn the heat to low and simmer for 15 minutes. Remove from the heat and let cool. Strain into a resealable container, discarding the solids. Store in the refrigerator for up to 2 weeks.

vanilla syrup

MAKES 1½ CUPS

1 teaspoon vanilla extract
1 cup granulated sugar

In a small saucepan over medium heat, combine the sugar, vanilla, and 1 cup water. Stir until the sugar is dissolved. Remove from the heat and let cool, then transfer into a resealable container. Store in the refrigerator for up to 2 weeks.

honey syrup

MAKES 1½ CUPS

1 cup honey
1 cup warm water

In a small bowl, whisk together the honey and warm water until the honey is dissolved. Store in a resealable container in the refrigerator for up to 4 weeks.

chai syrup

MAKES 1½ CUPS

1 bag chai
1 cup granulated sugar

In a small heat-resistant measuring cup, steep the chai in 1 cup hot water for 5 minutes. Remove the tea bag. Add the sugar and stir until dissolved. Transfer to a resealable container. Store in the refrigerator for up to 2 weeks.

stocking your bar cart for a holiday party

The key to stocking your bar cart for a holiday party is to select one to three signature cocktails and build your ingredient list around them. Trying to buy ingredients to make a large variety of cocktails can get cumbersome and downright expensive. So focusing on just a few staple drinks is easier and more budget-friendly. In addition to buying ingredients for your signature cocktails, you can add a few bottles of sparkling wine and some nonalcoholic alternatives for guests who don't consume alcohol.

christmas cookie board

Pair your favorite Christmas cookies with a cocktail for the most indulgent dessert that even Santa will appreciate. To create a Christmas Cookie Board, grab a large wooden board or serving platter, then lay out your favorite cookies—think chocolate chip cookies, shortbread cookies, sugar cookies, gingerbread cookies, linzers, oatmeal cookies, and/or peanut butter cookies. I recommend pairing them with spicy, warm drinks like the Spiced Orange Sipper (page 67), Old-Fashioned Toddy (page 99), or the Naughty List (page 129).

COCKTAIL RIMS

Adding a special rim to your cocktail glass is an easy way to elevate even the simplest drink. In order to rim a glass, generally speaking, you only need two ingredients: something to wet the glass and something to stick to the rim! Here are a few ideas to inspire your Christmas cocktail–making.

peppermint kiss rim

Honey or melted white chocolate
Finely crushed candy canes

Use it on: Peppermint Snowball (page 94)

Using a small food-safe paintbrush or a clean fingertip, add honey or melted white chocolate to the glass rim and set aside. Place crushed candy canes on a plate or in a shallow bowl. Take your prepared glass and dip it upside down onto the plate. Rotate the glass a few times so that the candy cane bits coat the entire rim.

golden rim

Honey
Edible gold flakes

Use it on: Winter Daiquiri (page 46), Beach Bitters (page 77), Cran-Ginger Punch (page 108)

Using a small food-safe paintbrush or a clean fingertip, add honey to the glass rim. Then, using tweezers or your fingers, place the gold flakes around the rim on top of the honey.

floral rim

Dried hibiscus leaves, finely chopped
Salt
Simple Syrup (page 20) or lime juice

Use it on: Hibiscus Honey Sour (page 50), Snow Day Sipper (page 135)

In a small bowl, combine the hibiscus leaves and salt.

Using a small food-safe paintbrush or a clean fingertip, add the simple syrup or lime juice to the glass rim and set aside. Place the hibiscus salt on a plate or in a shallow bowl. Take your prepared glass and dip it upside down onto the plate. Rotate the glass a few times so that the salt coats the entire rim.

sprinkle rim

Simple Syrup (page 20)
Holiday sprinkles

Use it on: Sugar Cookie Milk (page 53), Winter Warmer (page 90), Stocking Stuffer (page 122)

Using a small food-safe paintbrush or a clean fingertip, add simple syrup to the glass rim and set aside. Place sprinkles on a plate or in a shallow bowl. Take your prepared glass and dip it upside down onto the plate. Rotate the glass a few times so that the sprinkles coat the entire rim.

FESTIVE HOLIDAY GARNISHES

Garnishes always elevate the cocktail experience. Here are a few festive holiday garnishes that will impress your guests and take your cocktails to the next level.

sugared cranberries

MAKES ½ CUP SUGARED CRANBERRIES

½ cup fresh cranberries
½ cup Simple Syrup (page 20)
¼ cup granulated sugar

These cranberries make for a gorgeous garnish and a tasty snack. Add them to your favorite cocktail, charcuterie board, or dessert.

In a medium bowl, combine the fresh cranberries and simple syrup and toss to coat. Using a slotted spoon, remove the coated cranberries from the bowl and place them on a parchment paper–lined tray or cookie sheet to dry for 1 hour. Once the coated cranberries are dried and sticky, add them to a bowl with the sugar and toss to coat. Store in an airtight container in the fridge for 3 to 4 days.

sugared rosemary

MAKES 8 SUGARED ROSEMARY SPRIGS

8 rosemary sprigs
½ cup Simple Syrup (page 20)
¼ cup granulated sugar

I love using sugared rosemary sprigs to garnish my holiday cocktails. They look just like mini pine trees covered in snow and get me in the holiday spirit.

In a medium bowl, combine the rosemary sprigs and simple syrup and toss to coat. Using a slotted spoon, remove the coated rosemary sprigs from the bowl and place them on a parchment paper–lined tray or cookie sheet to dry for 1 hour. Once the sprigs are dried and sticky, add them to a bowl with the sugar and toss to coat. Store in an airtight container in the fridge for 3 to 4 days.

cocktail garnish board

An easy way to add a fun, interactive component to your holiday party is to let guests personalize their drinks with garnishes from a cocktail garnish board. This works especially well if you're serving a punch or batched cocktail. To set it up, pull out a wooden board or serving platter. Add chopped fresh fruit, fresh herbs, and serving utensils (e.g., tongs, picks, etc.). Then let your guests embark on their very own cocktail garnishing journey.

SCALING UP YOUR COCKTAILS

Batching is the process of taking cocktails from one serving to multiple servings in a few simple steps. This is especially helpful when hosting because it keeps you from getting stuck behind the bar making individual cocktails at your gathering.

All of the cocktails in this book can be batched if you follow these simple tips:

1. *Make sure you have the right tools.* Batched recipes require larger vessels for measuring and mixing. So having measuring cups, a pitcher, and a large spoon will make the process easier for you.

2. *Get your ratios right.* To make a balanced batched cocktail, scale up the recipe using the correct ratios. Start with the original single-serving recipe, then multiply each ingredient by the number of servings you want. For example, if a cocktail calls for 1 ounce of rum and you want to make 8 servings, simply multiply: 1 ounce × 8 = 8 ounces of rum for the batch. If math isn't your strong suit, you can also use an online recipe multiplier to check your work.

3. *Batch ahead.* If you're batching for an event or party, I recommend batching a day ahead of time if you can. That way, on the day of the party, you can focus on other tasks and you'll have more time to mingle with your guests.

4. *Don't forget to dilute.* When you batch a cocktail, you are missing out on the ice dilution that happens when you shake or stir a small-format drink with ice. Since water is an essential ingredient in creating a balanced cocktail, you'll want to ensure

you are adding some to your batch either when creating or serving. As a general rule of thumb, you should add ½ ounce water per serving to your batch. Keep in mind there's no need to add water if you've decided to add ice to your pitcher.

5. *Save the bubbles for serving.* For batched cocktails with ginger beer, sparkling water, sparkling wine, or any other bubbly ingredient, you'll want to avoid adding them to the batch too early so your drink doesn't go flat. I recommend either adding them to the batch right before serving or adding them directly to glasses at serving time.

holiday classics

FESTIVE TWISTS ON FAVORITE SIPS

sugar and spice margarita

• MAKES 1 DRINK •

The margarita is probably my favorite classic cocktail to remix. I love it because with just a simple substitution of the sweetener or the addition of a fun rim, this drink can be transformed into so many variations. Here, I've subbed out the classic simple syrup for a spiced version that has notes of brown sugar, ginger, cloves, and cinnamon. For the alcohol, I'm using reposado tequila, a tequila that's been aged in oak barrels at least 2 months, which gives it depth and warmth. The marriage of the spiced syrup with the aged tequila, along with the citrus elements, creates the perfect Christmas margarita.

THE RIM

1 tablespoon ground cinnamon
1 tablespoon granulated sugar
1 ounce freshly squeezed lime juice

THE DRINK

1½ ounces reposado tequila
1 ounce Spiced Syrup (page 20)
¾ ounce freshly squeezed lime juice
¾ ounce orange liqueur
1 cinnamon stick for garnish

Make the rim: On a plate or in a shallow bowl, combine the ground cinnamon with the sugar. Moisten the rim of a lowball glass with lime juice. Dip the glass upside down into the sugar mixture and rotate a few times so that the sugar coats the rim. Set aside.

Make the drink: In a cocktail shaker, combine the tequila, spiced syrup, lime juice, and orange liqueur and fill with ice. Shake until well chilled, about 10 seconds, then pour into the prepared glass. Garnish with a cinnamon stick.

mistletoe mojito

• MAKES 1 DRINK •

Decked out in red and green, this Christmas mojito is perfectly on theme with a red pomegranate juice base and green mint leaf embellishments. And not only does it look good, it tastes great too—bright, minty, and full of festive flavors that remind us of the holiday season.

6 mint leaves, plus more for garnish
1 ounce Simple Syrup (page 20)
1½ ounces white rum
1 ounce pomegranate juice
¼ ounce freshly squeezed lime juice
2 ounces club soda
Pomegranate arils for garnish

In a cocktail shaker, muddle together 6 mint leaves and the simple syrup until the mint is fragrant, then add the rum, pomegranate juice, and lime juice and fill with ice. Shake until well chilled, about 10 seconds, then double-strain into an ice-filled highball glass. Top with the club soda. Garnish with the remaining mint leaves and the pomegranate arils.

winter daiquiri

• MAKES 1 DRINK •

I often get asked what my favorite cocktail is. And my answer has been the same for years: the classic daiquiri. The original version is light, tart, and refreshing. This seasonal version is no different, with some fun additions. A spiced syrup dresses it up for the holidays, while the split base of dark rum and white rum adds a welcomed spice and sweetness.

1 ounce white rum
¾ ounce dark rum
1 ounce Spiced Syrup (page 20)
¾ ounce freshly squeezed lime juice
1 cinnamon stick or a dash of ground cinnamon for garnish
1 lime wheel for garnish

In a cocktail shaker, combine the white rum, dark rum, spiced syrup, and lime juice and fill with ice. Shake until well chilled, about 10 seconds, then strain into a coupe glass. Grate fresh cinnamon on top (or sprinkle ground cinnamon, if using) and garnish with a lime wheel.

nutty barista espresso martini

• MAKES 1 DRINK •

Espresso martinis are forever a moment. And if you think you've tasted every variation, think again. This one uses a pistachio syrup to add a salty, sweet, nutty twist that blends surprisingly well with the bitterness of the coffee. Mix that with the gorgeous and tasty white chocolate pistachio rim and you're in for an indulgent sipping experience. This one is perfect for after dinner when you need something to satisfy your sweet craving. You can find white chocolate syrup at any grocery or specialty beverage store.

THE RIM

- 2 tablespoons white chocolate syrup
- ½ cup pistachios, shelled and coarsely chopped

THE DRINK

- 1 ounce vodka
- 1 ounce Pistachio Syrup (page 21)
- 1 ounce white chocolate liqueur
- 1 ounce cold brew or espresso

Make the rim: On a plate or in a shallow bowl, add the white chocolate syrup. Dip the rim of your martini glass upside down into the syrup and rotate a few times so that the syrup coats the rim. Sprinkle the pistachios onto the coated glass, rotating to ensure coverage around the glass. Set aside.

Make the drink: In a cocktail shaker, combine the vodka, pistachio syrup, white chocolate liqueur, and cold brew or espresso and fill with ice. Shake until well chilled, about 10 seconds, then strain into the prepared glass.

hibiscus honey sour

• MAKES 1 DRINK •

I love making lemonades at home and infusing them with different syrups. I recently made a hibiscus lemonade that I absolutely loved. So why not turn it into a cocktail? Enjoy this tart and refreshing drink elevated with a sweet, floral syrup that brought a lot of excitement to my glass.

2 ounces gin
1 ounce Hibiscus Honey Syrup (page 22)
¾ ounce freshly squeezed lemon juice
1 lemon wheel

In a cocktail shaker, combine the gin, hibiscus honey syrup, and lemon juice and fill with ice. Shake until well chilled, about 10 seconds, then strain into a coupe glass. Garnish with a lemon wheel.

christmas paloma

• MAKES 1 DRINK •

The margarita gets a lot of attention. But the Paloma, a tequila cocktail typically made with grapefruit soda, is also worthy of the spotlight. It's one of my favorite tequila-based classics, and here I've added some holiday razzle-dazzle to it for a tasty holiday drink. It's sweet, tart, and bubbly. If you find the recipe to be too sweet or too tart, I recommend adding an ounce or two of sparkling water to taste.

3 ounces grapefruit soda
2 ounces blanco tequila
¾ ounce Spiced Cranberry Syrup (page 21)
¼ ounce freshly squeezed lime juice
Fresh or frozen cranberries for garnish

In a highball glass, combine the grapefruit soda, tequila, spiced cranberry syrup, and lime juice and fill with ice. Stir gently to combine and top with cranberries.

sugar cookie milk

• MAKES 1 DRINK •

Santa Claus has had enough cookies to last a lifetime. What he really wants is a sip of this boozy sugar cookie milk. He sees you when you're drinking and isn't judging. His only hope is that you've saved him a glass. Feel free to swap out the whole milk for a plant-based milk of your choice.

3 ounces whole milk
1½ ounces bourbon
½ ounce brandy
½ ounce Simple Syrup (page 20)
½ ounce amaretto
½ teaspoon vanilla extract
Rainbow sprinkles for garnish

In a cocktail shaker, combine the milk, bourbon, brandy, simple syrup, amaretto, and vanilla and fill with ice. Shake until well chilled, about 10 seconds. Pour into a lowball glass. Top with rainbow sprinkles.

toasted sleigh

• MAKES 1 DRINK •

Gather 'round the fire for a s'mores-flavored cocktail you'll never forget. Though this is a spirit-forward cocktail, the strength is balanced out by the sweetness of the toasted marshmallow syrup, the star of the drink. This syrup is an absolute game-changer that also tastes great as a sweetener in coffee, tea, and lattes.

2 ounces bourbon
¼ ounce Toasted Marshmallow Syrup (page 22)
3 dashes chocolate bitters
3 toasted marshmallows for garnish

In a mixing glass, combine the bourbon, toasted marshmallow syrup, and bitters and fill with ice. Stir until well chilled, about 15 seconds, then strain into an ice-filled lowball glass. Garnish with toasted marshmallows.

merry mule

• MAKES 1 DRINK •

If you like a Moscow mule, you'll be delighted by this cocktail. This variation uses cranberry juice to give it a holiday flair, with hints of whiskey and lime, and topped with the sweet heat of ginger beer, making everything feel merry and bright.

- 3 ounces ginger beer
- 1½ ounces whiskey
- 1 ounce cranberry juice cocktail
- ½ ounce freshly squeezed lime juice
- 1 lime wheel
- Fresh or frozen cranberries for garnish

In a lowball glass or copper mug, combine the ginger beer, whiskey, cranberry juice cocktail, and lime juice. Stir to combine. Garnish with a lime wheel and cranberries. Serve with a straw.

gingerbread man

• MAKES 1 DRINK •

The Gingerbread Man is sweet, spicy, and perfectly balanced, just like the beloved holiday treat. In case you needed more gingerbread vibes in your drink, the gingerbread cookie rim takes it to the next level. And now all I want for Christmas is this drink!

THE RIM

2 tablespoons honey
1 gingerbread cookie, coarsely chopped or crushed

THE DRINK

2 ounces vanilla vodka
1½ ounces Spiced Syrup (page 20)
1 ounce half-and-half
3 dashes aromatic bitters

Make the rim: On a plate or in a shallow bowl, add the honey. On another plate or in another shallow bowl, add the gingerbread. Dip the rim of your coupe glass upside down into the honey and rotate a few times so the honey coats the rim. Then dip the coated glass into the gingerbread, rotating to ensure coverage around the glass. Set aside.

Make the drink: In a cocktail shaker, combine the vodka, spiced syrup, half-and-half, and bitters and fill with ice. Shake until well chilled, about 10 seconds, then strain into the prepared coupe glass.

christmas in the tropics

DRINKS TO BANISH THE WINTER BLUES

sorrel coco sleigh

• MAKES 1 DRINK •

Growing up as the child of Caribbean immigrants, nothing signaled the start of the holidays for me more vividly than the sight of dried sorrel leaves—rich with color, scent, and tradition. Known commonly as hibiscus and by many other names across the African diaspora, sorrel is a vibrant red flower that's tart in flavor. In my culture, we use it to make a sweet drink by the same name. So this cocktail is a nod to a beloved traditional holiday drink, reimagined as a colada-style sip that's sure to sweep you off your feet.

2 ounces light rum
2 ounces pineapple juice
1½ ounces cream of coconut (see Notes)
½ ounce Sorel Liqueur (see Notes)
Pineapple wedge for garnish

In a cocktail shaker, combine the rum, pineapple juice, cream of coconut, and Sorel Liqueur and fill with ice. Shake until well chilled, about 15 seconds, then pour into a lowball glass. Garnish with a pineapple wedge.

NOTES This recipe calls for cream of coconut, not to be confused with coconut cream or coconut milk. I recommend Coco Lopez or Reál brands. Additionally, Sorel Liqueur is a hibiscus-flavored liqueur that can be found online or at your local liquor store.

santa's sipper

• MAKES 1 DRINK •

When you think tropical drinks, whiskey might be the last spirit that comes to mind. But in Santa's Sipper, the caramel and vanilla notes of the whiskey provide the perfect foundation for the other ingredients to shine. The addition of Campari provides a strong bitterness that creates a nice opposition to the sweet pineapple and simple syrup.

1 ounce whiskey
1 ounce pineapple juice
½ ounce freshly squeezed lime juice
½ ounce Campari
½ ounce Simple Syrup (page 20)
1 ounce sparkling water

In a cocktail shaker, combine the whiskey, pineapple juice, lime juice, Campari, and simple syrup and fill with ice. Shake until well chilled, about 10 seconds, then pour into a lowball glass and top with sparkling water.

spiced orange sipper

• MAKES 1 DRINK •

The Spiced Orange Sipper is like an elevated sidecar. The orange ginger syrup in this cocktail does most of the heavy lifting. That flavor is complemented by the cognac, adding notes of warmth, spice, and vanilla, while the citrus from the lemon juice cuts through with acidity and freshness.

2 ounces cognac
1 ounce Orange Ginger Syrup (page 27)
¾ ounce freshly squeezed lemon juice
Orange slice for garnish

In a cocktail shaker, combine the cognac, orange ginger syrup, and lemon juice and fill with ice. Shake until well chilled, about 10 seconds, then strain into a coupe glass. Garnish with an orange slice.

merry and bright mimosa

• MAKES 1 DRINK •

Growing up in New York, Christmas morning usually meant blustery winds and freezing temperatures. I've always wondered what it might be like to wake up on a beach instead—sun on my face, waves in the background, warmth in the air. This drink is that in a glass: a Christmas morning mimosa with a beachside twist.

2 ounces mango juice, chilled
1 ounce Basil Syrup (page 25)
3 ounces sparkling wine, chilled
Basil leaf for garnish

In a champagne flute, add the mango juice and basil syrup and stir gently to combine. Top with sparkling wine and garnish with a basil leaf.

diy mimosa bar

The DIY Mimosa Bar is the ultimate brunch party hack. It's an easy way to bring an interactive element to your next get-together while letting your guests play mixologist. To create it, you'll need:

- A few bottles of sparkling wine
- A selection of juices or fruit nectars
- Chopped or sliced fresh fruit for garnish
- Champagne flutes

To set up your bar, you'll want to find a table or countertop big enough to hold all your ingredients. Spread them out in the designated area and label them so ingredients are easy for guests to identify. I recommend using carafes or pitchers for the juices and nectars and bowls or small containers for the fruit. You can also include signage with instructions to guide guests through the mimosa-making process. From there, feel free to add other decorative finishing touches like fun paper straws, cocktail picks, etc., to make it festive.

mrs. claus' martini

• MAKES 1 DRINK •

Why should Mr. Claus get to have all the fun? The Mrs. Claus' Martini is the perfect marriage of ginger and mint. The ginger syrup provides a warm and spicy punch that's balanced out by the cool and refreshing sensation of the mint leaves. The candied ginger garnish provides a little more heat but is also a snack to munch on between sips.

4 to 6 mint leaves
¾ ounce Ginger Syrup (page 26)
2 ounces vodka
½ ounce orange liqueur
Candied ginger for garnish

In a cocktail shaker, muddle together the mint leaves and ginger syrup, then add the vodka and orange liqueur and fill with ice. Shake until well chilled, about 10 seconds. Double-strain into a martini or coupe glass. Garnish with the candied ginger on a cocktail pick.

coo-coo for coconuts

• MAKES 1 DRINK •

When it comes to tropical flavors, coconut is at the top of the list for me. It's my go-to flavor when I want to feel like I'm sipping on the beach without leaving the comfort of my living room. The Coo-coo for Coconuts transports you to the tropics with just three ingredients, including cream of coconut—a velvety, rich coconut syrup that adds hints of vanilla to set the vacation vibe. If you want to amp up the coconut flavor even more, substitute the white rum for a coconut rum.

1½ ounces white rum
¾ ounce freshly squeezed lime juice
½ ounce cream of coconut (see Notes, page 63)
Lime wheel for garnish
Coconut flakes for garnish

In a cocktail shaker, combine the white rum, lime juice, and cream of coconut and fill with ice. Shake until well chilled, about 10 seconds, then strain into a coupe glass. Garnish with a lime wheel and sprinkle coconut flakes on top.

beach bitters

• MAKES 1 DRINK •

In my experience, there's a perception that in order for a drink to be considered tropical, it has to be sweet or frozen. But that's not always the case. Beach Bitters has many elements that you would expect to find in a tropical drink, such as pineapple juice and lime juice, but the addition of amaro, a bitter herbal liqueur, cuts the sweetness and provides a nice balance and interest. I recommend using a brand that is fruitier and less bitter, like Amaro Nonino or Amaro Montenegro.

1½ ounces dark rum
1 ounce pineapple juice
1 ounce Cinnamon Syrup (page 25)
¾ ounce amaro
½ ounce fresh lime juice
Pineapple frond for garnish

In a cocktail shaker, combine the rum, pineapple juice, cinnamon syrup, amaro, and lime juice and fill with ice. Shake until well chilled, about 10 seconds, then pour into a lowball glass. Garnish with a pineapple frond.

elf elixir

• MAKES 1 DRINK •

Lychee is a small round tropical fruit native to China with a sweet and slightly floral flavor. Inspired by the ever-popular lychee martini, this twist uses coconut to soften the lychee and add a silky creaminess to the drink. It's important that you use canned peeled and pitted lychees for this recipe, not fresh; we use the syrup for the cocktail and garnish it with the whole lychees.

THE RIM

1 tablespoon honey
¼ cup toasted coconut flakes

THE DRINK

2 ounces blanco tequila
1 ounce lychee syrup from a can of lychees in syrup
½ ounce cream of coconut (see Notes, page 63)
½ ounce freshly squeezed lime juice
½ ounce orange liqueur
3 lychees for garnish

Make the rim: On a plate or in a shallow bowl, add the honey. On another plate or in another shallow bowl, add the toasted coconut flakes. Dip the rim of a lowball glass upside down into the honey and rotate a few times so the honey coats the rim. Then dip the coated glass into the coconut flakes, rotating to ensure coverage around the glass. Set aside.

Make the drink: In a cocktail shaker, combine the tequila, lychee syrup, cream of coconut, lime juice, and orange liqueur and fill with ice. Shake until well chilled, about 10 seconds, then pour into the prepared lowball glass. Garnish with the lychees on a cocktail pick.

reindeer refresher

• MAKES 1 DRINK •

This is an easy, refreshing cocktail to mix up when you don't have a lot of time but want something packed with flavor. The recipe calls for tequila but this is one of those recipes that works well with almost any spirit. You can even go spirit-free if you prefer; just leave out the tequila.

3 ounces ginger beer
2 ounces coconut water
1½ ounces blanco tequila
¾ ounce pomegranate juice
½ ounce fresh lime juice
Pomegranate arils for garnish

In a highball glass or copper mug, combine the ginger beer, coconut water, tequila, pomegranate juice, and lime juice and fill with ice. Stir to mix, then garnish with pomegranate arils.

beachside blush

• MAKES 1 DRINK •

Inspired by the cosmopolitan, I like to think that this is a tropical riff on the classic, with familiar ingredients like vodka, orange liqueur, and lime juice, while ingredients like cherry juice and mango juice give it a nice refresh. The perfect poolside sipper!

1½ ounces vodka
1 ounce tart cherry juice
1 ounce mango juice
½ ounce Simple Syrup (page 20)
½ ounce orange liqueur
½ ounce fresh lime juice
1 lime wheel for garnish

In a cocktail shaker, combine the vodka, cherry juice, mango juice, simple syrup, orange liqueur, and lime juice and fill with ice. Shake until well chilled, about 10 seconds, then strain into a coupe or martini glass. Garnish with a lime wheel.

warm up this winter

A MIX OF WARM DRINKS TO CURL UP WITH—NO YULE LOG NECESSARY

holly jolly steamer

• MAKES 1 DRINK •

There's nothing better than a hot, boozy drink to warm you from the inside out in the dead of winter. This spiced tea cocktail combines rich dark rum, bright citrus, and a gingery kick for a comforting sip that's both soothing and spirited. It's perfect for winding down after a chilly day or serving at a cozy gathering by the fire.

6 ounces hot water
1 bag black tea
1 ounce Orange Ginger Syrup (page 27)
1 ounce dark rum
¼ ounce freshly squeezed lemon juice
1 orange slice for garnish

In a heat-resistant cup, add hot water and the black tea. Let steep for about 3 minutes and discard the tea bag. Add the orange ginger syrup, rum, and lemon juice. Stir to combine, then garnish with an orange slice.

jingle jangle latte

• MAKES 1 DRINK •

The Jingle Jangle Latte reminds me of a warm apple pie. The spiced apple syrup mixed with the rich caramel notes in the cognac create a warm, dessert-like cocktail you'll want to sip all season and beyond.

6 ounces warm milk
2 ounces cognac
1 ounce Spiced Apple Syrup (page 27)
1 ounce espresso
Cinnamon stick for garnish

In a heat-resistant cup, add the milk, cognac, spiced apple syrup, and espresso. Stir to combine and garnish with a cinnamon stick.

winter warmer

• MAKES 1 DRINK •

For me, nothing screams winter more than hot chocolate. There's no beverage more comforting than a warm cup of rich hot chocolate on a frigid winter day. This recipe adds some interest in the form of white chocolate and vanilla vodka. I hope this one hugs you like a warm blanket. And make sure you don't skip the whipped cream!

8 ounces warm milk
1 ounce vanilla vodka
¾ ounce chocolate syrup
½ ounce white chocolate liqueur
Whipped cream for garnish

In a heat-resistant cup, add the milk, vodka, chocolate syrup, and white chocolate liqueur. Stir to combine and top with whipped cream.

warm christmas cider

• MAKES 1 DRINK •

This recipe is a great way to elevate a basic store-bought apple cider. A little bourbon and lemon juice go a long way to add more flavor to a beloved but basic fall and winter staple. Warm it up and you've got yourself the perfect cold-weather treat.

6 ounces apple cider, warmed
1½ ounces bourbon
¾ ounce freshly squeezed lemon juice
Apple slice for garnish
Cinnamon stick for garnish

In a heat-resistant cup, add the apple cider, bourbon, and lemon juice. Stir to combine and garnish with the apple slice and cinnamon stick.

peppermint snowball

• MAKES 1 DRINK •

Crème de menthe is a sweet mint-flavored liqueur that adds refreshing flavor to this drink. It comes in green and clear varieties, and to stay true to its name and preserve a clean, white, wintry appearance, the Peppermint Snowball is crafted with the clear version, but you can sub for the green version if that's what you have on hand, without changing the taste.

THE RIM

1 tablespoon honey
1 candy cane, finely crushed

THE DRINK

4 ounces warm milk
1 ounce crème de menthe
1 ounce reposado tequila
¾ ounce white chocolate liqueur
¼ ounce vanilla extract

Make the rim: On a plate or in a shallow bowl, add the honey. On another plate or in another shallow bowl, add the crushed candy cane. Dip the rim of a heat-resistant glass upside down into the honey and rotate a few times so the honey coats the rim. Then dip the glass upside down into the candy cane pieces and rotate a few times so that they coat the rim.

Make the drink: In the prepared glass, add the milk, crème de menthe, tequila, white chocolate liqueur, and vanilla. Stir to combine.

s'mores steamer

• MAKES 1 DRINK •

S'mores are one of my favorite sweet treats but making them at home can be quite an arduous task, especially if you don't have your own personal fire pit. So why not make them into a drink instead? The toasted marshmallow garnish is like a decadent cherry on top. For a richer, creamier version, use warm milk instead of water.

4 ounces hot water
1 ounce vodka
¾ ounce Toasted Marshmallow Syrup (page 22)
½ ounce chocolate syrup
1 marshmallow, toasted, for garnish

In a heat-resistant cup, stir together the hot water, vodka, toasted marshmallow syrup, and chocolate syrup. Garnish with a marshmallow.

buzzed bean

• MAKES 1 DRINK •

Your classic vanilla latte, all grown up. Personally, if you're not a huge coffee drinker like me, I'd opt out of the espresso in this one. But if you'd like a caffeine kick, 2 to 3 ounces should do the trick.

3 ounces warm milk
2 to 3 ounces espresso (optional)
1½ ounces bourbon
½ ounce Simple Syrup (page 20)
½ ounce Vanilla Syrup (page 28)

In a heat-resistant cup, stir together the milk, espresso (if using), bourbon, simple syrup, and vanilla syrup. Serve warm.

old-fashioned toddy

• MAKES 1 DRINK •

An Old-Fashioned, but make it "tea." Perfect for unwinding after a long day of wrapping presents, this delicious spiked "tea" has all the flavors of the classic Old-Fashioned cocktail in a super drinkable twist.

4 ounces hot water
2 ounces whiskey
½ ounce Simple Syrup (page 20)
3 dashes aromatic bitters
1 dash orange bitters

In a heat-resistant mug, stir together the water, whiskey, simple syrup, and bitters.

santa's spiced toddy

• MAKES 1 DRINK •

When I think of the holidays, I think of warm spices that make you feel like you're being wrapped in a warm, cozy blanket. My twist on a hot toddy does just that, using one of my favorite recipe hacks: a bag of chai brings as much spice as possible with minimal effort. Dark rum and honey are the perfect complement.

1 bag chai
6 ounces hot water
1 ounce dark rum
¾ ounce Honey Syrup (page 28)

In a heat-resistant cup, add the chai and water and let steep for 4 minutes. Remove the tea bag and add the rum and honey syrup. Stir to combine.

winter orchard

• MAKES 1 DRINK •

This hot toddy is an overload of all the incredibly juicy, flavorful citrus fruits that are at their peak freshness during the winter months. Think of it as your favorite hot toddy's bolder, more vibrant cousin.

6 ounces warm water
1 orange slice
1 grapefruit slice
1 lemon slice
1 ounce Spiced Apple Syrup (page 27)
1 ounce gin

In a heat-resistant glass, add the warm water, fruit slices, spiced apple syrup, and gin. Stir to combine and let steep for 5 minutes before enjoying.

party perfect punches

BATCHED COCKTAILS FOR SERVING A MERRY CROWD

tipsy santa

• MAKES 8 TO 10 DRINKS •

Inspired by my Jamaican roots, I love rum punch, and it's often the drink of choice at many family gatherings. I winter-fied it a bit by adding spice. The warm notes of cinnamon, cardamom, clove, and ginger in the chai add just enough spice to turn this summer staple into a Christmas-worthy sip.

3 cups chai, freshly brewed and chilled
2 cups dark rum
¾ cup orange juice
½ cup pineapple juice
¼ cup freshly squeezed lime juice
½ cup Simple Syrup (page 20)
⅛ cup aromatic bitters
Lime wheels for garnish
Cinnamon sticks for garnish

In a large pitcher, add the chai, rum, fruit juices, simple syrup, bitters, and ¾ cup water. Stir to combine. To serve, divide evenly among lowball glasses filled with ice and garnish each with a lime wheel and a cinnamon stick.

cran-ginger punch

• MAKES 6 TO 8 DRINKS •

This punch is fruit-forward and sweet, with a little kick provided by the ginger beer. If making ahead of time, save the ginger beer for serving so the bubbles don't go flat before your guests arrive.

1½ cups vodka
¾ cup cranberry juice
¾ cup pineapple juice
½ cup freshly squeezed lime juice
¼ cup Simple Syrup (page 20)
2 cups ginger beer
Candied ginger for garnish

In a large pitcher, stir together the vodka, fruit juices, simple syrup, and ½ cup water. To serve, divide evenly among lowball glasses filled with ice and top with ginger beer. Garnish each with candied ginger.

holiday party menus

Nothing goes better with a well-crafted meal than a perfectly paired cocktail. Here are some simple suggestions to inspire you to use the cocktails in this book to elevate your menu no matter the occasion.

- Having people over for brunch? Serve the Cherry Mint Sparkler (page 118) with a breakfast frittata.
- Hosting a dinner party? Pair the Santa's Sipper (page 64) with a roast or steak.
- Planning a cocktail party? Batch a few servings of the Sugar and Spice Margarita (page 42) ahead of time and pair with a grazing board stocked with meats, cheeses, and dried fruits.
- Looking for a nightcap that will warm you up and also satisfy your sweet tooth? Try pairing the Jingle Jangle Latte (page 89) with your favorite sweet treat.

yuletide yak punch

• MAKES 5 TO 6 DRINKS •

This punch is the perfect mix of two classic cocktails—a Manhattan and a sidecar. I love the warmth that the cognac and vermouth provide, while the lemon adds freshness to balance out the booze.

1½ cups cognac
½ cup sweet vermouth
½ cup Simple Syrup (page 20)
¼ cup fresh lemon juice
Lemon slices for garnish

In a large pitcher, stir together the cognac, sweet vermouth, simple syrup, lemon juice, and ½ cup water. To serve, divide evenly among lowball glasses filled with ice. Garnish each one with a lemon slice.

tinsel and tequila

• MAKES 6 TO 8 DRINKS •

The Tinsel and Tequila is sure to be a crowd-pleaser! The way the cinnamon syrup plays off the citrus in this cocktail is pure magic— comforting yet vibrant. The pinch of salt adds the perfect amount of brightness.

2 cups reposado tequila
1 cup Cinnamon Syrup (page 25)
½ cup freshly squeezed grapefruit juice
¼ cup freshly squeezed lime juice
Pinch of salt

THE RIM
2 tablespoons freshly squeezed lime juice
¼ cup salt, plus more as needed

In a pitcher, stir together the tequila, cinnamon syrup, grapefruit juice, lime juice, ½ cup water, and a pinch of salt. To serve, divide evenly among lowball glasses filled with ice.

Make the rim: Using a small food-safe paintbrush or a clean fingertip, add lime to the glass rim and set aside. Place salt on a plate or in a shallow bowl. Take your prepared glass and dip it upside down onto the plate. Rotate the glass a few times so that the salt coats the entire rim. Set aside until ready to serve.

santa-gria

• MAKES 6 TO 8 DRINKS •

The key to a great sangria is patience. Once you combine all the ingredients, you have to give them time to meld and marinate in the pitcher. And just like a good stew, the longer it sits the better it tastes.

One 750ml bottle red wine
¼ cup Orange Ginger Syrup (page 27)
¼ cup brandy
Juice of 1 lemon
1 lemon, sliced
1 orange, sliced, plus more slices for garnish
2 cloves

In a large pitcher, stir together the wine, orange ginger syrup, brandy, lemon juice, lemon slices, orange slices, and cloves. Refrigerate for at least 4 hours. To serve, divide evenly among lowball or wine glasses filled with ice. Garnish each one with an orange slice.

gingerbread punch

• MAKES 4 TO 6 DRINKS •

If you're too full for dessert but still want to satiate your sweet tooth, this flavorful punch just may be your answer. The half-and-half adds a little creaminess without having the drink feel heavy, making it the perfect post-dinner pour.

⅛ cup vanilla extract
1 cup Spiced Syrup (page 20)
1 cup half-and-half
1½ cups bourbon
Ground cinnamon for garnish

In a large pitcher, stir together the vanilla, spiced syrup, half-and-half, bourbon, and ½ cup water. To serve, divide evenly among lowball glasses filled with ice. Garnish each one with a sprinkle of ground cinnamon.

apple pie sangria

• MAKES 6 TO 8 DRINKS •

Sangrias are my favorite type of batched cocktail to make. They're easy to put together and a total crowd-pleaser. If you want to take the booze level up a notch, you can let your fruits soak in the brandy for an hour or so before adding them to the drink. Think of it like a little Christmas Eve treat for your fruits (and you)!

One 750ml bottle red wine
1 cup apple cider
¼ cup Spiced Apple Syrup (page 27)
¼ cup brandy
¼ cup freshly squeezed orange juice
Juice from 1 lemon
1 lemon, sliced
2 apples, chopped
3 cinnamon sticks
Apple slices for garnish

In a large pitcher, stir together the wine, apple cider, spiced apple syrup, brandy, orange juice, lemon juice, sliced lemon, apple, and cinnamon. Refrigerate for at least 4 hours. To serve, divide evenly among lowball or wine glasses filled with ice. Garnish each one with an apple slice.

cherry mint sparkler

MAKES 4 TO 6 DRINKS

This one is lighter on the alcohol but packs a real punch when it comes to flavor. It's a great option for brunch but can be served any time of day. The sparkling wine adds the bubbles I always crave during the holiday season.

- ½ cup blueberries, plus more for garnish
- 24 mint leaves, plus more for garnish
- ¾ cup tart cherry juice
- ½ cup orange liqueur
- ½ cup Simple Syrup (page 20)
- 3 cups sparkling wine

In a large pitcher, muddle together the blueberries and mint leaves. Add the cherry juice, orange liqueur, and simple syrup and stir gently to combine. To serve, divide evenly among champagne flutes and top each with sparkling wine. Garnish with mint and blueberries.

st. nick's vanilla cider

• MAKES 4 TO 6 DRINKS •

This is a really simple punch you can throw together if time is not on your side. It's sweet, refreshing, and familiar, and the vanilla is a delicious and unexpected accompaniment to the apple cider.

2 cups bourbon
2 cups apple cider
¾ cup Vanilla Syrup (page 28)
½ cup freshly squeezed lemon juice

In a large pitcher, stir together the bourbon, apple cider, vanilla syrup, lemon juice, and ½ cup water. To serve, divide evenly among lowball glasses filled with ice.

stocking stuffer

• MAKES 6 TO 8 DRINKS •

Though the Stocking Stuffer is creamy, it's surprisingly light and full of apple flavor. It uses Calvados, a French apple brandy made in Normandy. I loved using it alongside the apple cider because it adds an earthy, tart apple flavor.

2 cups apple cider
2 cups Calvados
1½ cups Irish cream (like Baileys)
1½ cups Cinnamon Syrup (page 25)
Cinnamon sticks for garnish

In a large pitcher, stir together the apple cider, Calvados, Irish cream, cinnamon syrup, and ½ cup water. To serve, divide evenly among lowball glasses filled with ice. Garnish each with a cinnamon stick.

naughty and nice

A COLLECTION OF
BOLD AND BOOZY COCKTAIL
RECIPES AND THEIR LOW-ABV
COUNTERPARTS

The Mint Tea-ni is bold with its split base of white and dark rum. The Under the Mistle-tea keeps things lighter but just as lively—the addition of sparkling water gives it a festive fizz that makes every sip feel like a party in a glass.

NAUGHTY

mint tea-ni

• MAKES 1 DRINK •

5 mint leaves
1 ounce Blackberry Syrup (page 26)
2 ounces brewed Earl Grey tea
1½ ounces white rum
½ ounce dark rum
½ ounce freshly squeezed lemon juice
2 ounces sparkling wine
Blackberries for garnish

In a cocktail shaker, muddle the mint with the blackberry syrup. Add the Earl Grey tea, white rum, dark rum, and lemon juice and fill with ice. Shake until well chilled, about 10 minutes. Strain into a highball glass and top with sparkling wine. Garnish with the blackberries and sugared rosemary sprig.

NICE

under the mistle-tea

• MAKES 1 DRINK •

5 mint leaves
1 ounce Blackberry Syrup (page 26)
2 ounces brewed Earl Grey tea
½ ounce white rum
½ ounce freshly squeezed lemon juice
2 ounces sparkling water
1 sugared rosemary sprig for garnish (page 35)

In a cocktail shaker, muddle the mint with the blackberry syrup. Add the Earl Grey tea, white rum, and lemon juice and fill with ice. Shake until well chilled, about 10 seconds. Strain into a highball glass and top with sparkling water. Garnish with the blackberries and sugared rosemary sprig.

Whether you're on Santa's naughty or nice list, you deserve a cocktail. And I've got one for you. For those on the Naughty List, you'll enjoy a rich, spirit-forward cocktail that's like a cinnamon Old-Fashioned made with a rich cinnamon syrup, whiskey, and orange bitters. On the Nice List, we're serving a lighter cinnamon-forward sour.

NAUGHTY

the naughty list

• MAKES 1 DRINK •

2 ounces whiskey
¼ ounce Cinnamon Syrup (page 25)
3 dashes orange bitters
1 cinnamon stick for garnish

In a mixing glass filled with ice, add the whiskey, cinnamon syrup, and bitters. Stir to combine, about 15 seconds. Strain into a lowball glass with fresh ice. Garnish with a cinnamon stick.

NICE

the nice list

• MAKES 1 DRINK •

1½ ounces whiskey
1 ounce Cinnamon Syrup (page 25)
¾ ounce lemon juice
1 sugared rosemary sprig (page 35)
1 cinnamon stick for garnish

In a cocktail shaker, combine the whiskey, cinnamon syrup, and lemon juice and fill with ice. Shake until well chilled, about 10 seconds, then pour into a lowball glass. Garnish with a sugared rosemary sprig and cinnamon stick.

MERRY CHRISTMAS
MERRY CHRISTMAS

take-home cocktails

Give your guests a small token to remember your party by giving them a pre-mixed cocktail bottled in a mason jar or swing-top bottle to take with them when they leave. Take-home cocktails can be made ahead of time so they're ready when guests are leaving (see page 11 for more on gifting cocktails). They can be a signature drink recipe from the party or something new and exciting. Either way, they make a great gift and ensure that your loved ones think of you and your celebration long after it's over. Who doesn't like a souvenir?

Tinsel on the Rocks and the Tinsel Spritz are party-perfect drinks with unexpected flavors. The marriage of blueberry and vanilla in both drinks is next-level rich and completely irresistible. While the Tinsel Spritz takes a more restrained approach when it comes to alcohol content, the Tinsel on the Rocks shows just how bold it can be with the addition of tequila.

NAUGHTY

tinsel on the rocks

• MAKES 1 DRINK •

- 8 blueberries, plus more for garnish
- ¾ ounce Vanilla Syrup (page 28)
- 2 ounces blanco tequila
- ½ ounce orange liqueur

In a cocktail shaker, muddle the blueberries with the vanilla syrup. Add the tequila and orange liqueur and fill with ice. Shake until well chilled, about 10 seconds, then pour into a lowball glass. Garnish with the remaining blueberries.

NICE

tinsel spritz

• MAKES 1 DRINK •

- 8 to 10 blueberries, plus more for garnish
- ¾ ounce Vanilla Syrup (page 28)
- ½ ounce orange liqueur
- 3 ounces sparkling wine, chilled

In a champagne flute, muddle the blueberries with the vanilla syrup. Add the orange liqueur and sparkling wine. Stir gently to combine. Garnish with the remaining blueberries.

Each of these cocktails—the Snow Day Sipper and the Snow Day Sparkler—feature a gorgeous hibiscus honey syrup, which gives them a rich, vibrant red hue. The Snow Day Sipper keeps things bold and interesting—perfect for a holiday party—while the Snow Day Sparkler has less alcohol but makes up for it with ginger beer, which provides both fizz and flavor.

NAUGHTY

snow day sipper

• MAKES 1 DRINK •

2 ounces vodka
1 ounce freshly squeezed lemon juice
1 ounce Simple Syrup (page 20)
½ ounce Hibiscus Honey Syrup (page 22)

In a cocktail shaker, combine the vodka, lemon juice, simple syrup, and hibiscus honey syrup and fill with ice. Shake until well chilled, about 10 seconds, then strain into a coupe glass.

NICE

snow day sparkler

• MAKES 1 DRINK •

1 ounce vodka
1 ounce lemon juice
1 ounce Simple Syrup (page 20)
½ ounce Hibiscus Honey Syrup (page 22)
3 ounces ginger beer

In a cocktail shaker, combine the vodka, lemon juice, simple syrup, and hibiscus honey syrup and fill with ice. Shake until well chilled, about 10 seconds, then strain into a highball glass. Top with ginger beer.

The Yuletide Espresso Martini is anything but ordinary—think your favorite espresso martini dressed up in its holiday best with spicy chai and sweet white chocolate. The bold and boozy version goes all-in with a triple threat of coffee liqueur, rum, and white chocolate liqueur. But don't let the low-ABV counterpart, A Very Chai Christmas, fool you—it still delivers that rich, cozy coffee flavor, just gentler on the alcohol.

NAUGHTY

yuletide espresso martini

• MAKES 1 DRINK •

1 ounce cold brew or espresso
1 ounce coffee liqueur
1 ounce dark rum
½ ounce Chai Syrup (page 28)
½ ounce white chocolate liqueur
2 espresso beans for garnish
Star anise for garnish

In a cocktail shaker, combine the cold brew, coffee liqueur, rum, chai syrup, and white chocolate liqueur and fill with ice. Shake until well chilled, about 10 seconds, then strain into a coupe glass. Garnish with the espresso beans and star anise.

NICE

a very chai christmas

• MAKES 1 DRINK •

1 ounce cold brew or espresso
1 ounce coffee liqueur
¾ ounce amaro
½ ounce Chai Syrup (page 28)
½ ounce white chocolate syrup
2 espresso beans for garnish
Star anise for garnish

In a cocktail shaker, combine the cold brew, coffee liqueur, amaro, chai syrup, and white chocolate syrup and fill with ice. Shake until well chilled, about 10 seconds, then strain into a coupe glass. Garnish with the espresso beans and star anise.

index

A

alcohol, low-AVB cocktails. *See* nice-list cocktails
apples/apple cider
  Apple Pie Sangria, 117
  Spiced Apple Syrup, 27
  St. Nick's Vanilla Cider, 121
  Stocking Stuffer, 122–*123*
  Warm Christmas Cider, *92*, 93

B

bar spoon, 15
bar, stocking for holiday parties, 29
Basil Syrup, 25
batching cocktails, 37–38. *See also* punches
Beach Bitters, *76*, 77
Beachside Blush, 82–*83*
berries
  Blackberry Syrup, 26
  Cran-Ginger Punch, 108–*109*
  Spiced Cranberry Syrup, 21
  Sugared Cranberries, 34
  Tinsel on the Rocks, 132–*133*
bitters, beach, *76*, 77
Blackberry Syrup, 26
bourbon
  Buzzed Bean, 98
  Gingerbread Punch, 116
  St. Nick's Vanilla Cider, 121
  Sugar Cookie Milk, *52*, 53
  Toasted Sleigh, 54–*55*
  Warm Christmas Cider, *92*, 93
Buzzed Bean, 98

C

Calvados, in Stocking Stuffer, 122–*123*
chai. *See* tea
champagne flutes, 16
Cherry Mint Sparkler, 118–*119*
chocolate
  S'mores Steamer, *96*, 97
  Winter Warmer, 90–*91*
chocolate, white and white chocolate liqueur
  Nutty Barista Espresso Martini, *48*, 49
  Peppermint Kiss Rim, 31
  Peppermint Snowball, 94
  A Very Chai Christmas, 136
  Winter Warmer, 90–*91*
  Yuletide Espresso Martini, 136
Christmas cocktails. *See also* classic holiday cocktails; naughty-list cocktails; nice-list cocktails; punches; tropical drinks; warm drinks; *specific main alcohol ingredients*
  about: Christmas Cookie Board and, 30; recollections of Christmas dinner and, 9; stocking your bar for party, 29; this book and, 10
  batching, scaling up for volume, 37–38
  garnishes, 34–36
  gifting cocktails, 11
  glassware for, 16–19
  party menus, 109
  rims for glasses (*See* rims, cocktail)
  take-home cocktails, 131
  tools for making, 15–16, 37
  welcome cocktails, 14
Christmas Cookie Board, 30
Christmas Paloma, 51
cider. *See* apples/apple cider

Cinnamon Syrup, 25
citrus
  Orange Ginger Syrup, 27
  Spiced Orange Sipper, *66*, 67
citrus press, 15
classic holiday cocktails, 41–59
  Christmas Paloma, 51
  Gingerbread Man, 58–*59*
  Hibiscus Honey Sour, 50
  Merry Mule, *56*, 57
  Mistletoe Mojito, *44*, 45
  Nutty Barista Espresso Martini, *48*, 49
  Sugar and Spice Margarita, 42–*43*
  Sugar Cookie Milk, *52*, 53
  Toasted Sleigh, 54–*55*
cocktail rims. *See* rims, cocktail
cocktail shaker, 15
coconut
  Coo-coo for Coconuts, 74–*75*
  Elf Elixir, 78–*79*
  Sorrel Coco Sleigh, *62*, 63
coffee liqueur. *See also* espresso
  A Very Chai Christmas, 136–*137*
  Yuletide Espresso Martini, 136–*137*
cognac
  Jingle Jangle Latte, *88*, 89
  Spiced Orange Sipper, *66*, 67
  Yuletide Yak Punch, *110*, 111
Coo-coo for Coconuts, 74–*75*
cookie board, Christmas, 30
copper mugs, 16
cosmopolitan-inspired drink. *See* Beachside Blush
coupe glasses, 19
cranberries. *See* berries
crème de menthe, in Peppermint Snowball, 94

D

daiquiri, winter, 46–*47*
dinner party menus, 109. *See also* Christmas cocktails; punches

E

Elf Elixir, 78–*79*
espresso
  about: sweetener for (*See* Toasted Marshmallow Syrup)
  Buzzed Bean, 98
  Jingle Jangle Latte, *88*, 89
  Nutty Barista Espresso Martini, *48*, 49
  A Very Chai Christmas, 136
  Yuletide Espresso Martini, 136

F

festive glassware, 17
Floral Rim, 32

G

garnishes, 34–36
  about: garnish board for guests, 36
  Sugared Cranberries, 34
  Sugared Rosemary, 35
gifting cocktails, 11
gin
  Hibiscus Honey Sour, 50
  Winter Orchard, 103
ginger
  Ginger Syrup, 26
  Gingerbread Man, 58–*59*
  Gingerbread Punch, 116
  Orange Ginger Syrup, 27
ginger beer
  Cran-Ginger Punch, 108–*109*
  Merry Mule, *56*, 57
  Reindeer Refresher, *80*, 81
  Snow Day Sipper, *134*, 135
  Snow Day Sparkler, *134*, 135
glass, mixing, 16
glassware
  festive, tips for creating, 17
  rim a glass, 31
  types of, 16–19
Golden Rim, 31

H

heat-resistant glasses, 19
Hibiscus Honey Sour, 50
Hibiscus Honey Syrup, 22
highball glasses, 19
holiday party menus, 109. *See also* Christmas cocktails
Holly Jolly Steamer, 86–*87*

honey
- Hibiscus Honey Sour, 50
- Hibiscus Honey Syrup, 22
- Honey Syrup, 28

hot toddies. *See* warm drinks

I

Irish cream, in Stocking Stuffer, 122–*123*

J

jigger, 15
Jingle Jangle Latte, *88*, 89

L

lattes. *See* espresso
low-ABV cocktails. *See* nice-list cocktails
lowball glasses, 19

M

Manhattan. *See* Yuletide Yak Punch
margarita, sugar and spice, 42–*43*
marshmallows
- S'mores Steamer, *96*, 97
- Toasted Marshmallow Syrup, 22
- Toasted Sleigh, 54–*55*

martini glasses, 19
martinis
- Mrs. Claus' Martini, *72*, 73
- Nutty Barista Espresso Martini, *48*, 49
- Yuletide Espresso Martini, 136

menus, holiday party, 109
Merry and Bright Mimosa, 68–*69*
Merry Mule, *56*, 57
mesh strainer, 16
milk
- Buzzed Bean, 98
- Jingle Jangle Latte, *88*, 89
- Peppermint Snowball, 94
- Sugar Cookie Milk, *52*, 53
- Winter Warmer, 90–*91*

mimosas
- DIY Mimosa Bar, 71
- Merry and Bright Mimosa, 68–*69*

mint
- Cherry Mint Sparkler, 118–*119*
- Mint Tea-ni, 126–*127* (*See also* Under the Mistle-tea)
- Peppermint Kiss Rim, 31
- Peppermint Snowball, 94

Mistletoe Mojito, *44*, 45
mixing glass, 16
mojito, mistletoe, *44*, 45
Moscow Mule. *See* Merry Mule
Mrs. Claus' Martini, *72*, 73
muddler, 16
mule. *See* Merry Mule
multiple cocktails, batching, 37–38

N

naughty-list cocktails
- Mint Tea-ni, 126–*127*
- The Naughty List, *128*, 129
- Snow Day Sipper, *134*, 135
- Tinsel on the Rocks, 132–*133*
- Yuletide Espresso Martini, 136

nice-list cocktails
- bold counterparts (*See* naughty-list cocktails)
- The Nice List, *128*, 129
- Snow Day Sparkler, *134*, 135
- Tinsel Spritz, 132–*133*
- Under the Mistle-tea, 126–*127*
- A Very Chai Christmas, 136

Nutty Barista Espresso Martini, *48*, 49

O

Old-Fashioned Toddy, 99
orange. *See* citrus

P

Paloma, Christmas, 51
parties, holiday. *See also* Christmas cocktails; classic holiday cocktails; naughty-list cocktails; nice-list cocktails; punches; tropical drinks; warm drinks; *specific main alcohol ingredients*
- garnish board for guests, 36 (*See also* garnishes)
- menus for, 109
- stocking your bar for, 29
- take-home cocktails, 131

peppermint. *See* mint
Peppermint Snowball, 94
Pistachio Syrup, 21
pitchers, 19
punches, 105–123
about: batching cocktails, 37–38; ice dilution and, 37–38; sparkling/bubbly ingredients and, 38
Apple Pie Sangria, 117
Cherry Mint Sparkler, 118–*119*
Cran-Ginger Punch, 108–*109*
Gingerbread Punch, 116
Santa-gria, *114*, 115
St. Nick's Vanilla Cider, 121
Stocking Stuffer, 122–*123*
Tinsel and Tequila, 112–*113*
Tipsy Santa, 106–*107*
Yuletide Yak Punch, *110*, 111

R

red wine glasses, 19
Reindeer Refresher, *80*, 81
rims, cocktail, 31–33
about: overview of, 31
Floral Rim, 32
Golden Rim, 31
Peppermint Kiss Rim, 31
Sprinkle Rim, 32
rosemary, sugared, 35
rum, dark
Beach Bitters, *76*, 77
Holly Jolly Steamer, 86–*87*
Tipsy Santa, 106–*107*
Yuletide Espresso Martini, 136
rum, white/light
Coocoo for Coconuts, 74–*75*
Mint Tea-ni, 126–*127*
Mistletoe Mojito, *44*, 45
Sorrel Coco Sleigh, *62*, 63
Under the Mistle-tea, 126–*127*
Winter Daiquiri, 46–*47*

S

sangria. *See* wine, red
Santa-gria, *114*, 115
Santa's Sipper, 64–*65*
Santa's Spiced Toddy, 100–*101*
shaker, cocktail, 15
sidecar. *See* Spiced Orange Sipper; Yuletide Yak Punch
Simple Syrup, 20
sleigh, toasted, 54–*55*
Snow Day Sipper, *134*, 135
Snow Day Sparkler, *134*, 135
Sorrel Coco Sleigh (with Sorel Liqueur), *62*, 63
Spiced Apple Syrup, 27
Spiced Cranberry Syrup, 21
Spiced Orange Sipper, *66*, 67
Spiced Syrup, 20
spiced toddy, Santa's, 100–*101*
Sprinkle Rim, 32
St. Nick's Vanilla Cider, 121
Stocking Stuffer, 122–*123*
stocking your bar for parties, 29
strainer, mesh, 16
Sugar and Spice Margarita, 42–*43*
Sugar Cookie Milk, *52*, 53
Sugared Cranberries, 34
Sugared Rosemary, 35
syrups
about: rim glasses using, 32 (*See also* rims, cocktail)
Basil Syrup, 25
Blackberry Syrup, 26
Chai Syrup, 28
Cinnamon Syrup, 25
Ginger Syrup, 26
Hibiscus Honey Syrup, 22
Honey Syrup, 28
Orange Ginger Syrup, 27
Pistachio Syrup, 21
Simple Syrup, 20
Spiced Apple Syrup, 27
Spiced Cranberry Syrup, 21
Spiced Syrup, 20
Toasted Marshmallow Syrup, 22
Vanilla Syrup, 28

T

tea. *See also* Old-Fashioned Toddy
Chai Syrup, 28
Holly Jolly Steamer, 86–*87*

Mint Tea-ni, 126–*127*
Santa's Spiced Toddy, 100–*101*
Tipsy Santa, 106–*107*
Under the Mistle-tea, 126–*127*
A Very Chai Christmas, 136
Yuletide Espresso Martini, 136
tequila, blanco
Christmas Paloma, 51
Elf Elixir, 78–*79*
Reindeer Refresher, *80*, 81
Tinsel on the Rocks, 132–*133*
tequila, reposado
Peppermint Snowball, 94
Sugar and Spice Margarita, 42–*43*
Tinsel and Tequila, 112–*113*
Tinsel and Tequila, 112–*113*
Tinsel on the Rocks, 132–*133*
Tinsel Spritz, 132–*133*
Tipsy Santa, 106–*107*
Toasted Marshmallow Syrup, 22
Toasted Sleigh, 54–*55*
tools, for creating cocktails, 15–16, 37
tropical drinks, 61–83
Beach Bitters, *76*, 77
Beachside Blush, 82–*83*
Coo-coo for Coconuts, 74–*75*
Elf Elixir, 78–*79*
Merry and Bright Mimosa, 68–*69*
Mrs. Claus' Martini, *72*, 73
Reindeer Refresher, *80*, 81
Santa's Sipper, 64–*65*
Sorrel Coco Sleigh, *62*, 63
Spiced Orange Sipper, *66*, 67

V

vanilla cider, St. Nick's, 121
Vanilla Syrup, 28
A Very Chai Christmas, 136
vodka
Beachside Blush, 82–*83*
Gingerbread Man (vanilla vodka), 58–*59*
Mrs. Claus' Martini, *72*, 73
Nutty Barista Espresso Martini, *48*, 49
S'mores Steamer, *96*, 97
Snow Day Sipper, *134*, 135
Snow Day Sparkler, *134*, 135
Winter Warmer, 90–*91*

W

Warm Christmas Cider, *92*, 93
warm drinks, 85–103
Buzzed Bean, 98
Holly Jolly Steamer, 86–*87*
Jingle Jangle Latte, *88*, 89
Old-Fashioned Toddy, 99
Peppermint Snowball, 94
Santa's Spiced Toddy, 100–*101*
S'mores Steamer, *96*, 97
Warm Christmas Cider, *92*, 93
Winter Orchard, 103
Winter Warmer, 90–*91*
welcome cocktails, 14
whiskey
Merry Mule, *56*, 57
The Naughty List, *128*, 129
The Nice List, *128*, 129
Old-Fashioned Toddy, 99
Santa's Sipper, 64–*65*
white chocolate. *See* chocolate, white and white chocolate liqueur
wine, red
about: red wine glasses, 19
Apple Pie Sangria, 117
Santa-gria, *114*, 115
wine, sparkling
Cherry Mint Sparkler, 118–*119*
DIY Mimosa Bar, 71
Merry and Bright Mimosa, 68–*69*
Mint Tea-ni, 126–*127*
Tinsel Spritz, 132–*133*
Winter Daiquiri, 46–*47*
Winter Orchard, 103
Winter Warmer, 90–*91*

Y

Yuletide Espresso Martini, 136
Yuletide Yak Punch, *110*, 111

TEN SPEED PRESS
An imprint of the Crown Publishing Group
A division of Penguin Random House LLC
1745 Broadway
New York, NY 10019
tenspeed.com
penguinrandomhouse.com

Typefaces: Adobe's Caslon, Commercial Type's Graphik, and Din Studio Windey Signature

Library of Congress Cataloging-in-Publication Data

Names: Wilson, Camille (Writer on cocktails) author
Title: Christmas cocktails / by Camille Wilson.
Identifiers: LCCN 2025036952 (print) | LCCN 2025036953 (ebook)
ISBN 9780593840030 hardcover | ISBN 9780593840047 ebook
Subjects: LCSH: Cocktails | Christmas cooking
Classification: LCC TX951.2 .W55 2026 (print) | LCC TX951.2 (ebook)
LC record available at https://lccn.loc.gov/2025036952
LC ebook record available at https://lccn.loc.gov/2025036953
Hardcover ISBN 978-0-593-84003-0
Ebook ISBN 978-0-593-84004-7

Editor: Dena Rayess | Production editor: Serena Wang
Designer: Isabelle Gioffredi | Art director: Kelly Booth
Production manager and prepress color manager: Jane Chinn
Prop stylist: Yasna Glumac | Food stylists: Neetu Laddha and Mariana Swedelson
Copy editor: Sasha Tropp | Proofreaders: Rita Madrigal and Alison Kerr Miller
Publicist: Soren Eversoll | Marketer: Emily Hotaling

Manufactured in India

10 9 8 7 6 5 4 3 2 1

First Edition

The authorized representative in the EU for product safety and compliance is Penguin Random House Ireland, Morrison Chambers, 32 Nassau Street, Dublin D02 YH68, Ireland, https://eu-contact.penguin.ie.